MW00679233

# Dedication

This book is dedicated to two men who have both transitioned into the ancestral realm: My brother Jonathan Marcus Adell and my best friend James E. Quickley Jr. Their energy will forever live on and guide me towards fulfilling my purpose. This one's for you fellows!!!

This book is also written for my children: Ahsha, Chrislyn, and Jayden Adell; to help them deal with their mental health and understand my journey.

Lastly, I want to thank all the people who supported me along my journey. There are too many to name; family, friends, and co-workers.

ISBN: 978-1-63625-006-9 (Paperback Edition)
ISBN: 978-1-63625-007-6 (E-book)
Director of Photography: Nikalya Shodeen-Segura
Editor-in-Chief: Obieke Writes LLC
Main Website: www.untitledproductionteam.com/book

Special discounts on bulk quantities of UPT Publishing books are available to corporations, professional associations, colleges, universities, schools, churches, and other organizations. For more details, contact UPT directly.

Special Sales Department:
E-mail: cadell@uptsites.com

# TABLE OF CONTENTS

# LOVE WILL CONQUER ALL

"Love is an action." - Jonathan Marcus Adell

**A**ll of us struggle with fear and worry

from time to time. Fear is a reaction in our mind; it is not a physical thing we can hold. Therefore, fear can be an illusion of the mind but should not be confused with danger. Danger assessing risk and possible harm, distress, or jeopardy of one's safety. Fear and mental health have been linked in several ways because fear is an emotion. The word emotion represents energy in motion, and fear is one of the most powerful emotions we can give off. As adolescents, we learn that energy is neither lost nor destroyed, but instead only transferred from one party to the next. So, when we enter an emotional state of fear, where does this energy go? I will answer this question later in this book and show you the connection between fear and mental health, including the ways to identify, manage, and even overcome your deepest fears.

In our society, fear is embedded in the social construct we operate and is used to set boundaries within our minds. Some would consider fear a means to control the mind, while others might say it is a natural mental process that keeps us balanced. Let's examine this theory and draw a clear line between *fear* and *danger*.

Fear is a perception-based conclusion tethered to our senses (touch, taste, hearing, sight, smell, and thought). In contrast, **danger is a perspective-based conclusion formulated from reliable data from a particular viewpoint.** Further, while fear focuses on the longevity of one's experiences, danger assesses the immediate situation. Danger causes us to wear a seatbelt when we get into a car because of the number of traffic accidents that happen every day. At the same time, fear, which often involves our past experiences, adds to our perception of the current situation. For example, I have an aunt who never drives on the highway because an 18-wheel truck almost ran her off the road when she first began driving, and that experience added to how she perceives driving. Have you ever heard the saying, **"Perception is reality?"** This idea stems from the fact that we create or shape our reality, and anything the mind creates can become real to us. An individual feels this reality personally, but remember that fear is an energy that can be transferred to others.

Aaron Stalker, at the time a 28-year-old Army veteran, received a call from his girlfriend, who screamed, "There have been shots fired. Mom is shot!" What was the first emotion that Aaron's girlfriend invoked? Although it could easily be fear, it was love. **Love is the great equalizer** that allowed him to fight through the fear and look past the danger. **When dealing with mental health in 2020 and beyond, love is our greatest ally.** While others fled the Las Vegas shooting scene, Aaron drove straight into it to help hundreds of people to safety in pursuit of his loved ones. I had the pleasure of serving with Sergeant Stalker, who cared about people above all else. He always put people first despite what was happening around him. He embodied the mindset that if you take care of the people around you, the mission will always be complete.

It's natural to be concerned about our health, bank account, job status, children, and so on. When something threatens one of those areas, we take notice; hence, we work hard to protect ourselves and those we love. In some ways, fear is both a natural and helpful emotion, but only if it is rooted in love and compassion.

Love keeps our fear in control instead of allowing it to control us. **If our fear gets out of control, it can take over and prevent us from enjoying life.**

When consumed by fear, we can't be present for others or do the things we love. Overwhelming fear affects our health, both mentally and physically. It saps our strength, makes it difficult to concentrate, and robs us of sleep. Fear also keeps us from taking any risks. If we are afraid, we won't start new businesses, write books, or initiate relationships. We'll continuously play it safe, always trying to insulate ourselves from any negative consequences. **When we play it safe, we don't grow; we stagnate and miss out on great opportunities.**

We can't run from fear or simply hope it goes away. There will always be something to worry about and things we must manage. Pain is temporary, but it will almost always lead to mental health issues when suppressed. Avoidance is not a way out; it will only compound the pain, making it harder and harder to bear.

In 2020 and beyond, with a rise in human consciousness, we shift into a new paradigm that forces us to deal with ourselves and rediscover who we indeed are. *Mental Health Now* serves as a prelude to the challenges that we face during a global pandemic that induces prolonged fear. The first step in moving forward is accepting that we are all dealing with some sort of mental health issue, and just as we are concerned with our physical health, we cannot overlook our mental health.

This book will outline 11 techniques we can use to personally deal with mental health in 2020 and beyond. We will also explore the connection between fear and mental health and learn ways to identify, manage, and even overcome our deepest fears. To successfully navigate the often-difficult world we live in, we need effective strategies for coping with worry and fear. We must be able to deal with our anxieties in healthy and productive ways. Suppressed pain leads to mental health issues that generate fear and worry. Over time, our suppressed pain causes stress, and when left untreated, leads to severe mental health issues.

# What Exactly Is Fear?

"Our deepest fear is not that we are inadequate. Our deepest fear is that we are powerful beyond measure." – Marianne Williamson

Let's break this down. Fear is:

- **A biological response to an internal or external stimulus.** When you are afraid, your body goes into "fight or flight" mode. Your heart rate goes up, and your adrenaline increases. Your brain starts to race, and you may begin to sweat. All these things together create the emotion of fear.

- **A psychological response to an internal or external stimulus.** Fear can arise from within or from an outside factor. For example, thinking about losing your job (an internal stimulus) causes fear. Coming face-to-face with a grizzly bear (an external stimulus) also causes fear.

When dealing with your struggles, **it is essential to understand the source of your fear.** Is it arising internally or coming from an external source?

What you'll probably discover is that most of your fears are internal. You will very rarely find yourself in an actual life-or-death situation.

Typically when you are afraid, it's the result of what you *think* will happen rather than what is happening.

Furthermore, the majority of our fears aren't connected to reality. What we feel is real, but the circumstances causing these feelings are not factual. The fundamental truth is that **fear is mostly a response to an *imagined* reality.**

For example, let's say you find a strange lump on your neck. Immediately, you begin to fear the worst and think that you have cancer. But are you sick? Well, you won't know until you see the doctor, and she examines the symptoms. Yet you're still afraid. You worry in response to your imagination. Mark Twain summarized this experience best when he said, "I've had a lot of worries in my life, most of which never happened."

**When you understand the true nature of fear, it becomes easier to overcome.** You can closely examine your anxiety and determine if there is any substance to it. Some of your worries may have merit, but you'll discover that most of them do not. And even the ones that do, they probably aren't nearly as bad as you imagine.

Marianne Williamson famously posed the question, "What is our greatest fear"? She eloquently offered this statement in response, "Our deepest fear is not that we are inadequate. Our deepest fear is that we are powerful beyond measure". Indeed, fear holds us back from living life to the fullest. We must learn how to overcome our fears, so we can move toward the things we desire.

**In this guide, you'll discover proven strategies for facing and overcoming your fears.** You'll learn practical, healthy strategies for handling worry and anxiety. Will your fears suddenly vanish? No. But this book will equip you with many tools you need to face your fears and deal with them. Moreover, you'll be able to identify mental health issues in yourself and others before they become unmanageable.

*Are you Ready? Let's dive in.*

∴

I joined the U.S. Army in 2004, to the surprise of everyone I knew except for my father. **My mother told me that I was too talented to join the military.** Her words provided me with so much motivation and confidence because I knew she was right. From the beginning of my career, I never allowed my military experiences to change how I valued myself. I knew that I would continue to do great things after my service was complete. Growing up in the inner-city streets of New York, I understood danger and, as a product of my environment, I habitually normalized completely unacceptable behaviors.

For many of us, the first sign of an underlying mental health issue is the normalization of situations that should not be considered normal. For example, a child who continuously sees his parents argue and fight, and then over time is no longer bothered by this behavior, has developed a rewired mind or is desensitized to harsh realities. The majority of mental health issues are rooted in a person's adverse childhood experiences.

**I can say from my own experiences that poverty and mental illness are entangled or directly connected.** The connection between poverty and mental illness is called the *scarcity factor*. When someone is deprived of their basic needs for a prolonged period, anxiety, stress, and fear are driven into their subconscious mind and normalized. This theory is embedded in the marketing process called *scarcity value*. Consider this: Why are the most expensive sneakers, Air Jordans, also the best selling sneakers in low-income communities? The scarcity factor occurs when retailers release 200 pairs of Jordans, and in response, folks line up at malls for days trying not to miss out. Mentally, they feel as if they've been left out for so long, and a pair of sneakers—which they don't need—can subconsciously be compared to the lack of shelter or food they're experiencing. We sometimes feel valued by attaching ourselves to something of value. Again **love is the great equalizer** or self-love in this situation.

My mother planted seeds of self-love inside my heart that have allowed me to overcome mental illness in my early childhood despite coming from humble beginnings.

I found out very early on in my military career that a love like that was rare and invaluable. The military's recruitment process is comparable to what young men experience when recruited into a gang. Both the military and street gangs target young boys and men from either broken homes or from families with a member who has already joined the organized group. Although the goals of these organizations are different, the direct recruits share a likeness. This early observation helped me to gain a clear understanding of how to influence people. I recognize the difference between a person who joins the military because their father served compared to the person who joined because they wanted a father or big brother figure. I handle each situation differently when encountering these recruits.

**Teenagers and young adults who are dealing with mental health issues don't always have the tools needed to manage stress.** Typically, they manage stress in three major ways (either one or a combination of any three); sex, alcohol/drug abuse, or violent/reckless behavior. When I first joined the military, I managed my stress with all the above in excess. Before joining the military, I had one sexual relationship, although she did not know that she was my first. I had never used drugs or drank alcohol, and I was an accomplished student-athlete who played basketball 24/7. With the severe change in my environment (after joining the military) and the new stress of preparing myself for war while dealing with toxic leadership, I had easily succumbed to unhealthy means of managing my anxiety.

As a 21-year-old man, I had frequent sex with various partners and drank alcohol to the point where I was too intoxicated to drive. At times, I was a willing passenger in a vehicle with someone who had also had too much to drink. On numerous occasions, while hanging out at nightclubs with friends, we would get into trivial fights over small infractions. And over time, I learned to play all the card and dice games and eventually started gambling for recreation. Gambling fueled my competitive nature as a student-athlete like an addiction. In due time, this reckless behavior put me in financial quicksand; I found myself in a cycle of taking out payday loans with extremely high-interest rates. While all of this was happening, I knew my behavior was unacceptable. **Yet, I felt stuck because I didn't want to ask for help,** and I didn't know how to *effectively* manage my mental health and deal with the stress I was facing.

OK, now let's have a candid conversation about this. **The problem is children don't always learn from their parents healthy ways to deal with stress.** Reflect on your own experiences as a teenager or a young adult and consider these questions:

- How did you manage your mental health?
- Was it even thought about as a point of concern?
- What was your primary concern when faced with stressful situations?

For me, it was the possibility that the stress, the fear, or the pain would never end. Once we adopt the mindset that nothing will ever change a bad situation, our mental health has been adversely impacted by our environment. **As leaders and parents, we must be fully aware of the signs of hopelessness; it is a byproduct of fear and is very contagious.**

In the next chapter, I will outline some techniques you can implement in your daily life to help you deal with stress and face your fears. Changing your environment refers to changing the way you think. You should never normalize pain.

## **REFLECTION EXERCISE**

1. What are you afraid of? *List as many fears as possible.*

2. Is this fear internal or external? *Write down next to the fear which one it is.*

3. What is the source of your fear, where did it come from, or when did it come about? *Dig deep to get to the root of it.*

# CHANGE YOUR ENVIRONMENT

"Pain is temporary. It may last a minute, or an hour, or a day, or even a year. But eventually, it will subside. If I quit; however, it will last forever." – Eric Thomas

compound the effects of mental stress.

Consistently practicing these strategies will put you in a better position to manage your mental health, anxieties, and fears.

Physical activity is one of the primary ways young adults deal with mental health issues. Therefore, it is imperative to never take the joy out of exercising. Physical exercise is a much better option than excessive sex, alcohol, drug abuse, or violence.

## Unhealthy Coping Strategies
Multiple sex partners
Excessive ejaculation
Drug abuse
Excessive alcohol use
Emotional eating (bulimia and binging)
Violent or reckless behavior
## Healthy Coping Strategies
Eat and sleep well
Competitive sports/exercise
Progressive Muscle Relaxation (PMR)
Mediation (includes yoga)
Supportive people/healthy relationships
Tantra (semen retention)

# **REFLECTION**

1. How much *enjoyable* exercise do you get each day?

2. List three people or situations that bring you the most happiness? *What type of relationship are they (i.e., family, partner, etc.)?*

3. List three people or situations that drain you? *What type of relationship are they (i.e., family, work, etc.)?* What method do you use most to deal with your stress (i.e., sex, alcohol, etc.)?

# Knowing thyself!
"No one know you, more than you"

Before you can overcome mental stress, you must identify it. In other words, you have to name the source or root cause of your trauma. If you're not clear on the source of your fear or trauma, then you'll struggle to resolve it.

**To identify your trauma and fear. Ask yourself these questions:**

- What trauma am I dealing with?
- Why am I afraid of it?
- What do I try not to think about?
- When do I feel stressed or afraid?
- What emotions do I feel about myself?
- What adverse outcomes am I envisioning?
- What pictures do I have in my head about this situation?

You may need to work a bit to get to the bottom of your trauma. **It's common to have smaller trauma layered on top of much larger trauma from the same root cause that triggers you.**

For example, say you're afraid of losing your job. Is that the ultimate fear? Probably not. More likely, you're worried about not having enough money to pay bills or losing the respect of your peers when forced to restart your career.  Let's go deeper into our fears. Maybe we don't have the confidence to pursue our dreams of being an entrepreneur mainly because other people don't believe in those dreams or believe that it would be an unsuccessful means to make a living.

When identifying your fears, keep pushing until you get to the root cause. Work to determine the root fear that is causing all your other anxieties. Keep asking yourself, "So what?"

For example:

- So, what if I lose my job? *I won't make any money.*
- So, what if I don't make any money? *I can't pay the bills.*
- So, what if I can't pay the bills? *I can't provide for my family.*

Dig until you determine the real reason why you're afraid.

**Next, become aware of all the different ways your fear is affecting your life.** Does it

- Cause you constant emotional distress?
- Keep you from doing things you want to do?
- Hamper your relationships?
- Hurt your work performance?
- Steal your happiness?
- Prevent you from enjoying the present?

The goal of this exercise is to bring you face-to-face with the consequences of your fear. When you see how the worry and anxiety damage your life and hold you back, you become much more motivated to take action.

It may help you to write out your thoughts as you work through the above processes. Writing things down helps you think clearly and forces you to voice your anxious thoughts and feelings.

**You can't avoid your fear. The more you try to ignore it, the more it will grow. The only way to move forward is to look it in the eye.** Confront your fears face-to-face and put a name to them. Then you can begin to dismantle them.

∴

The turning point of my life happened on December 10, 2005—a day that I will never forget. We discussed my self-destructive behavior in the previous chapters, but let me explain how it all changed. After a very long week of working 12-hour shifts, I would go out clubbing with my friends. My ritual was getting off work at 6 P.M., taking a nap from 7 P.M. -10:30 P.M., and then waking up to get ready to go to the club before midnight. I did this on both Friday and Saturday, staying out until about 5 A.M. each night.

Yet December 10th was different because my alarm didn't go off that night, so I slept through the night completely. On Saturday morning, I woke up to 16 messages from my best friend, James, who I partied with every weekend. I tried to call James back, but he didn't answer, so I got dressed and went to basketball practice at the gym. I played for the Fort Bliss post basketball team, and despite my late-night activities, I always made it to practice on Saturday mornings at 8:30 A.M. As practice was ending, my squad leader (who was also a good friend of mine) walked into the gym. I saw him and immediately thought, *I hope I don't have to go to work*. I could never prepare myself for what he had to say. He told me that James was killed by a drunk driver that night while leaving the club.

At first, I felt guilt—and not because I had somehow caused James' death—but because I believed that I could have prevented it. The loss of a loved one is a critical point in our life when we begin to reflect on and evaluate our mental health. Grieving is a natural process, but everyone grieves in their own way and on their timeline. However, when death triggers a negative emotion like guilt, fear, jealousy, or hate, we must immediately check on our mental health and stability. I held on to this guilt for months, going into a deep state of depression, and no level of assistance could help me.

The individual who killed James was a staff sergeant in the army, and at the time, James and I were both junior enlisted Soldiers. James was married with three kids, but his family never received federal life insurance because he was driving while under the influence of alcohol. No one punished the noncommissioned officer for his crime. Although the collision itself was not 100% his fault, he was under the influence of alcohol, so I completely blame him. Over time, my guilt grew into anger, and I lost faith in the system and myself. I began to drift into a hollow place of hopelessness where all I could hear was my mother's voice saying, "Get out, you are too talented."

I began to go into a deep state of reflection to get to the root cause of the guilt I felt; I recognized that I should've felt blessed that I overslept and was not in the car with James that night. I was single with no kids, and James was married with three young children. He was my best friend, but when I began to evaluate my behavior as a friend, I saw the lack of genuine friendship I displayed toward James. **This reflection goes back to the last thing my little brother told me before he died last year, "Love is an action word."** Sometimes we say something like "this person is my best friend," but if we do not display the characteristics that make up this title, these words hold no value. A real friend would not have told a friend to start an argument so that he had an excuse to go out to the club. A real friend would have held him accountable and supported him as he worked through his marital issues. A real friend is not an enabler, and that was precisely what I had become.

Let's define the word friend because this type of relationship is the foundation of all human connections. A friend is defined as a person you know and have a bond of mutual affection or esteem. **As friends, leaders, and parents, we must accept that we cannot pull others out of this state of depression.** We can only create a positive environment around them to operate in as they take that journey inward. When you create a safe environment for them to heal and provide them with the genuine support they require, they will have the space needed to do the necessary inner work. If we try to force the process and control the outcome with judgment, our efforts will backfire. I am not saying give up on them, but it's important to accept that the work is theirs to get through. During this process, unauthentic support will be easily recognized and could damage your long-term relationship.

In the next chapter, we will explore ways we can shift our mindset when faced with obstacles. This practice will allow us to face our fears head-on.

Below are common types of depression you may see in yourself and others:

# Types of Depression

**Major depression** is characterized by an intense feeling of sadness.

**Bipolar disorder** is a brain disorder that causes an unusual shift in a person's mood.

**Dysthymic disorder** is a less intense type of depression, but it may persist for a long time.

**Psychotic depression** includes some features of psychosis, such as hallucinations or delusions.

**Adjustment disorder** occurs when an individual responds to a stressful event.

**Postpartum depression** is a form of depression that occurs after giving birth.

**Seasonal Affective Disorder (SAD)** is a type of depression that comes on in the winter months when the sun is sparse.

# Positive Affirmations vs Negative Affirmations

"Watch your self-talk, what you put after I am is key"

Considering the worst and best-case scenarios can dramatically alter your perspective and give you much-needed clarity about your fears.

**When you feel afraid, think about the worst-case scenario.** If everything went wrong, what is the worst that could happen? Now, what are the odds of that scenario happening? Probably pretty low. The worst-case scenario very rarely happens.

For example, say you're afraid of public speaking. The worst that could happen is you freeze up on stage, unable to speak, and as a result, you're humiliated. But will that happen? Almost certainly not. And even if it did, would it be that bad? Sure, you'd be embarrassed, but that's about it.

When you engage in worst-case thinking, you'll often discover that the worst isn't nearly as bad as you think it is. Therefore, worst-case thinking enables you to move forward and overcome your fears.

**After thinking through the worst-case, think through the best-case.** If everything goes well, what awesome things will you experience?

Instead of freezing on stage, you'll knock it out of the park. Your speech results in a standing ovation, you receive tons of compliments, and you get invited to speak at other events. Your confidence goes through the roof.

When you envision the good things that will come your way, it motivates you to take action in the face of your fears. You can see what you will miss out on if you let your worries control you.

Will everything go perfectly? Probably not. But the reality is that **everything doesn't have to go perfectly for you to reap the benefits of taking action.**

Now, to be clear, there may be times when the worst-case scenario is horrible, like with the diagnosis of an illness. In these scenarios, it can be especially helpful to think about the best-case situation. If things go well, you'll still have many years of life to enjoy with your family. Our minds are powerful beyond measure, so we must pay attention to the things we believe. Beliefs are like the police of the mind, and once our mind accepts these beliefs as truths, they become our reality. When a doctor tells you that you only have three months to live, you can choose to believe in the medical system that gives him authority to render that statement or face the fact that he is not the creator. Mental slavery is when you feel you don't have a choice. Yet, you can choose to believe the doctor or consider his statement as an opinion. Ask yourself, how many times a doctor has told someone they would never survive a serious illness or accident, yet the person lives. Your willingness to never quit is the human variable that can change your outcome. Be very mindful of how you perceive information that is not yet grounded in facts. Instead, focus on the best-case scenario; this can give you the strength you need to keep moving forward.

∴

"Friends, how many of us have them?" If people are the most significant energy source in our diet, then it is vital to understand the most important relationship you will have in life— friendship. Friendship should be at the core of any strong relationship. If you are married, your partner should be your friend first. If you have children, your children should also consider you to be their friend, especially once they become an adult. The old mentality that I am not my child's friend hinders many parents from genuinely getting to know their children and often ruins the possibility of fostering friendship when their child grows up. The strongest family relationships are rooted in friendship. What's the difference between your favorite cousin and all the others? Friendship. It is even necessary with a relationship between a leader and his subordinates. All fruitful relationships must be rooted in friendship, even if a lifelong friendship never blossoms.

We have heard that the people working for us should not be our friends, but this detachment and superiority concept creates the opportunity for toxic leadership to grow. To play devil's advocate, the way some people define friendship would not be a good way to lead others. Think about this, look at all the leaders you've worked for in your life and consider the best one; even after you stopped working for them, could you now consider them your friend? The truth is they've always been your friend without defining your relationship as a friendship. My first squad leader was my friend, and he still is today.

Good leaders are also good friends. I learned this lesson from James. Less than two years in the Army, and I already received a powerful life lesson that changed how I looked at the idea of friendship and amplified my ability to influence and motivate others. After James' funeral, I cried harder than I ever cried before, and it wasn't because of his funeral or tragic death. At the end of the ceremony, while everyone walked past his family to give their condolences, I realized something that broke my heart. I'd known James for a few years and called him my best friend, but I didn't even know his wife or children. His wife didn't even recognize me. After all of my time knowing him, I had wondered if I was truly even a friend. The answer was clear; I was not a good friend—I was an enabler.

Enablers disguise themselves as friends in hopes of being accepted, protected, loved, or comforted. You can be a sibling enabler, a parent enabler, a spouse enabler, and so on. Enabling creates an illusion of friendship when it's tethered to a strong societal title like a parent; it can be a weapon others use to destroy themselves. **When you are experiencing mental health issues or self-hatred, you love people who maintain you**

**in your self-destruction, and more often than not, your friends are your worst enemies.** Enablers in your life could unconsciously be your worst enemies because they allow you to destroy yourself, something a real friend would never do.

Let's examine this further. As an enabler, I would justify James' reasons for going out to the club with me every weekend. I would allow him to drive drunk, knowing that I wasn't willing to drive while under the influence of alcohol, and I would keep him out until the break of dawn without even thinking about his family. Remember, I didn't even allow myself to get to know his family, so I subconsciously wouldn't have to deal with the guilt. The same rules apply to leadership; when someone has a problem with leading their friends, they were never really a friend in the first place. When individuals go from being enablers and then try to become an effective leader, this creates serious conflict.

I am grateful to have learned this lesson before being put into a leadership role. I experienced zero challenges in all of my transitions into higher positions within the military. My colleagues were happy that I received these promotions over other individuals. After James' death, I promised myself that I would always maintain a great friend's qualities in every relationship that I built in the future.

I can look back at my life so far and see the fruits of my good friendships. I specifically recall a Soldier I went to military service school with back in 2010. He had just experienced four tough years under incredibly toxic leadership and expressed his disgust with the Army to me daily. I befriended him, and I can say today that he is one of the most powerful turnaround stories of my career without a shadow of a doubt. The irony of his story is that despite his initial dissatisfaction with the military, he became an Army Recruiter and not just any recruiter. He was ranked as the top recruiter on the East Coast, helping others change their lives. I do not credit myself for any of his accomplishments; he possessed all the tools he needed to succeed when I first met him. Yet, I provided him with something that so many leaders overlook, friendship.

When you hear the words "man's best friend," what is the first thing that comes to mind? We are not always put into situations where we can have a real friendship. Some people find that emotional support animals (or comfort pets) such as a dog can be of great benefit. Dogs release a hormone associated with happiness and affection. Therefore, they help decrease mental illness symptoms and assist by providing a sense of focus and purpose, improving self-esteem. Both dogs and humans are social creatures so the relationship is mutual. Comfort pets would be an excellent option for an adolescent who is dealing with depression or anxiety. Also, if you have a young child dealing with mental stress due to isolation and lockdown, getting them a pet that fits their age and responsibility level could help. I encourage you to do more research on emotional support animals to explore how they might personally help you deal with emotional and mental stress.

A good, healthy friendship that doesn't cross the line of being inappropriate for the time and situation is critical to building meaningful and lasting relationships. Friendship should be at the root of all good relationships, whether it is a partner, a parent, a coach, a mentor, a co-worker, a supervisor, a child, or any other family member. The qualities and attributes of a good friend amplify the top qualities of a good leader.

Below are nine of the most common qualities of both good friends and good leaders.

| Good Friend | Good Leader |
|---|---|
| Cares about you | Shows empathy |
| Shared Trust | Mutual loyalty |
| Mutual respect | Mutual respect |
| Supportive | Motivational |
| Honesty | Candid |
| Dependable | Responsible |
| Good listener | Active listener |
| Non-judgemental | Fair and impartial |
| Similar Interest | Common goals |

# TRUST THE PROCESS
"Faith without work is dead"

How much time and energy do you spend worrying about things you can't control? If you're like most people, you probably spend a lot of time worrying. After all, a considerable portion of life is out of your control, and if you focus on those things, you'll be constantly worried.

**For the most part, you can't control:**

- The actions and responses of others
- Local and global events
- Traffic
- Weather
- What others think
- Aging
- People's opinions of you
- The past
- The inevitability of death
- And a whole lot more!

Worrying about the things you can't control puts undue mental stress on you. It literally won't change a thing. And what's worse, it can divert your focus from the things you actually *can* control. When you fear things outside of your control, you have less energy to use in areas you can make a difference.

**What can you control?**

- How you respond to situations
- What you think about
- The ways you treat others
- The information you consume
- How you treat your body
- Your self-talk
- Your sleep habits
- How consistent you are
- And much more

**When you focus on what you can control, your fears will significantly decrease, and your life will dramatically improve.**

Think of it in terms of American (NFL) football. A defensive back can't control where the quarterback throws the football, but he can control his response to the throw. The more the defensive back focuses on how he will respond, the better he'll play.

The same is true in life. You can't control a significant portion of what happens, but you do have power over how you respond. The more you focus on your actions and thoughts, the better things will go for you.

**When you find yourself dealing with fear, stop and ask yourself, "*What things are under my control?*"**

Once you identify those things, give all your time and energy to them. Avoid spinning your wheels over things you have no control over. Turn your fears into action.

∴

There was a point in my life where I truly began to learn how I influenced others, and because of it, I gained a supreme level of confidence. **You cannot become an effective leader if you don't understand people.** Before you can learn about others, you must first know *thyself*. Self-reflection is a constant state of growth that allows you to deal with stress in real-time. Webster's Dictionary defines *self-reflection* as "mediation or serious thoughts about one's character, actions, and motives."

I adopted the mindset that **even if it was not my fault, it was always my responsibility to fix the situation** I found myself in. Many times when we feel something is not our fault, it's easy to defer the responsibility of changing the circumstances. For example, if you have a toxic leader at work who is continuously bullying and publicly humiliating you, is it your fault? No, but it is not a reasonable solution for you to wait until this toxic leader changes their behavior. You have to take action whether it's your fault or not. The military helped me learn this lesson. Yet, many people do not adopt this mindset as it requires a level of personal accountability. Remind yourself that the journey is a marathon, not a sprint. Growth takes time.

I was 33 years old at the apex of my career when this lesson really sank in. I was dealing with a lot of stress in my life and felt like I was losing control. Whether I was to blame or not, I had to hold myself accountable, and it was not easy. I went 18 months without seeing my son due to circumstances outside of my control. I had fallen into a state of hopelessness again. Yet, this time around, I didn't revert to unhealthy ways of managing my stress. I began to heal through others.

Trusting the process is a mantra that I adopted to steer myself away from the helpless mindset that people often adopt when things get out of control. Trusting the process helped me embrace my journey and recognize that any obstacle that presented itself in my life was not there to stop me but redirect me to my true purpose. **The universe means no ill will to me, and I mean no ill will to it.** Karma is not bad; it is merely the results of the Law of Attraction. The Law of Attraction means whatever you put out in the universe will come back to you. In the bible, Matthew 7:1-5 (New World Translation) expresses this idea when it says:

*"Stop judging that you may not be judged for with the judgment you are judging, you will be judged, and with the measure that you are measuring out, they will measure out to you. Why, then, do you look at the straw in your brother's eye but do not notice the rafter in your own eye? Or how can you say to your brother, 'Allow me to remove the straw from your eye,' when look! a rafter is in your own eye? Hypocrite! First remove the rafter from your own eye, and then you will see clearly how to remove the straw from your brother's eye."*

In 2015, I led a team of nine Soldiers into the Middle East, and before departing, I gave each one of them a book to read that had a particular lesson I felt they could learn. This team was one of the most diverse groups of soldiers I had ever seen come together. Each one of them was dealing with some deep pain, and I felt it. I was given the responsibility of leading this team at the last minute, but I knew the mission was for me because I saw myself in each of them.

Once we reached the Middle East, I asked each soldier for their parent's contact information. I spoke with all of their parents, expressing my commitment to take care of their children. Without any doubt, I knew that each Soldier would return home a better person than when they left. Because I knew they were all dealing with some level of pain, I had to understand them on a deeper level than just their job title.

A mentor helped me formalize the understanding of a process I call the *five fingers of human relationships*. Look at your hand and hold it in the air. There are five major components of human roles represented by looking at your hand. Each finger represents a part of your body and also a human role you carry in life. The thumb is the social title or profession you work in, and it is associated with the brain. The thumb stands out because it's uniquely positioned away from the other fingers. It is attached to our purpose in life, but keep in mind that a job title can be very trivial and does not always define our true purpose.

The next four fingers are positioned based on how an individual's life is structured. The middle finger is more pronounced, not just because of its size, but for its position at the core of our existence. It represents the heart and is the most agile finger on the hand. Typically this is where a father or mother's human role goes due to the responsibility connected to that role.

The pinky finger is the most fragile and usually represents the human role carrying the most insecurities or the role you feel you have the least control over. The pinky within the body represents the digestive system, which teaches us about faith, trust, and forgiveness. Typically, you can place the son or daughter role here because when a child comes into this world, they don't have a belief system; their parents are like gods. **Much is learned from a**

**parent but no more important lesson than faith, trust, and forgiveness.**

The ring finger has the least mobility of any finger on the hand and is usually glamourized in our lives because of its secure location paired next to the middle finger—"West Side." The ring finger represents our hormones, making it a primary place for the husband or wife's human role. The index finger is the human role that is judged or defined the most by others. This finger represents the liver and gallbladder, which means this finger is about filtering out toxins. Typically, this is where the man or woman role is placed as gender roles shape the way we think collectively. When one of these roles is damaged, broken, or vacant, it makes the entire hand more vulnerable. Once we gain a greater perspective on life, we see that each finger works collectively to help the hand operate. Try to isolate your finger by pushing that finger toward your palm and see how well the other fingers operate without it. Repeat this exercise for each finger.

Let's compare this theory to my deployment team of eight Soldiers. Five of them had two vacant human roles, which made them the most vulnerable in stressful environments. One of these Soldiers lost a grandparent who served in a fatherly role. So I did everything in my power to get him back home because he would have gone from 3 out of 5 human roles (or 60%, which is already low) to 2 out of 5 (40%). This level of instability in a hostile environment would have put him in a high-risk category.

I used the five finger process to manage the teams that I put together and dig deeper to better understand how vital each role was to them. I had another Soldier who had 5 out of 5 human roles filled, so you couldn't see much vulnerability on the outside. Once you connect with people personally, you understand the vulnerabilities they have in these roles and what role each finger represents. It is very easy for a soldier to put the marriage role on their pinky instead of their ring finger because they're often away from home. The love and support from a spouse are distant, like the love of a parent.

Have you ever broken a finger? Do you know how painful that is? There are levels to this process because not every wound heals the same. A finger can get cut off instantly, or the pressure from a known source can break it. This analogy is used here to help you better understand that the healing process is different, both physically and mentally, based on what takes place. Seeing your finger ripped off of your body has a different psychological effect on you than an injury due to impact. **While the physical healing process has a general healing timeline, the mental healing process does not.** Separation is challenging, whether it is a finger or a marriage, but how this separation or relationship breaks down is the key to understanding the mental health impact.

If someone with 5 out of 5 intact human relationships goes through a divorce, the separation could impact their relationship with their kids. This change would take them down to 3 out of 5 human relationships (a 40% loss). Although others entered the deployment environment with 60% connection, suffering a 40% loss in connection could pose a greater risk. It would be like walking around with two broken fingers. Also, consider that our identity as a man or woman is connected to some of our relationships. So how these relationships end can also impact how we view ourselves in these roles. Breakups due to infidelity hit us harder.

# COLLATERAL BEAUTY
"What you seek, you shall find."

Fear is almost always rooted in a scarcity mentality. In other words, you are afraid that you won't have something you want or desire.

**You're afraid that you'll lack:**

- Love
- Respect
- Money
- Health
- Possessions
- Or something else

These are all good things, and it's not wrong to desire them. But it's easy to become so fixated on these things that you become fearful of not having them.

**Gratitude completely shifts your perspective, fixing your gaze on the things you already have.** It's hard for gratitude and fear to coexist. They're like oil and water. A study of breast cancer patients corroborated this idea when it found that people "who intentionally practiced gratitude were much less likely to experience anxiety" (Otto et al., 2016).

When fear starts to rise in you, embrace gratitude. Look for ways to be grateful that are specifically related to your anxiety.
Are you worried about a medical condition? Express gratefulness for the health care available to you. Are you concerned about losing your job? Express gratitude for the chance to find something even better.

Every new day, one of the nation's top life and business strategists, Tony Robbins, focuses on gratitude. He says:

> *I focus on three moments in my life that I'm grateful for, because gratitude is the antidote to the things that mess us up. You can't be angry and grateful simultaneously. You can't be fearful and grateful simultaneously. So, gratitude is the solution to both anger and fear, and instead of just acting grateful, I think of specific situations that I'm grateful for, little ones and big ones. I do it every single day, and I step into those moments and I feel the gratitude and the aliveness.*

When you're consistently grateful, it's hard to be fearful. You're more aware of the good things you have.

**Some simple ways to practice gratitude include:**

- Keep a daily gratitude journal.
- Send a weekly text message of gratefulness to a friend.
- Send out handwritten notecards once a month.
- Tell your loved ones *why* you love them.
- Embrace every challenge as an opportunity to grow.
- Post about gratefulness on social media.

Optimism is a powerful thing, and there is no reward in pessimism. If you seek to find something wrong with a situation, you will surely find it.

∴

I always look for collateral beauty during any hardship. COVID-19 has swept the globe, taking away lives, jobs, and opportunities to connect with others. Yet, it also afforded me more time to spend with my children and heal myself. During this time, I have reflected on James' untimely death and all the negative emotions I felt that led to a nine-month adjustment disorder. In 2007, the year following his death, I won the Soldier of the Month Award, Soldier of the Quarter Award, and Soldier of the Year Award. And later that year, my superiors promoted me to the rank of a sergeant. I went from casually being in the Army to becoming the Army and dedicating my career to helping others find their path. I made a promise to myself to build a genuine connection with everyone I led. I grew to understand that success is not healing; it is a temporary relief from the mental stress we experience. Unless you assert the necessary measures to recover, no healing will get done.

Christopher Wallace, aka Biggie Smalls, said it best, "More money, more problems." In some situations, the more success you gain, the easier it becomes to bury your problems until they pour over into all areas of your life.

During these moments of success, we have mental momentum to focus our energy inward to heal. This task was easier said than done because I still had some maturing to do within myself.

One quote I remember hearing from my mother throughout my childhood still resonates with me today, "Treat people how you want to be treated." It was simple and direct, and most importantly, it required reflection in every action. Anybody with kids can relate to a moment when you asked your child why they did something, and they'd reply, "I don't know." Impulsive behavior leads to unnecessary baggage and regret. 2020 has carried us into a new paradigm, and the old ways of thinking must die to usher in the new world mindset. The concept of being your own worst critic is not healthy. The bible reminds us that, "What you seek, you shall find," so if you are looking for a flaw, you will indeed find one.

With stress, worry, and anxiety on the rise, we have to create healthy mental spaces by releasing undue pressure. We need to watch our self-talk because the words we put after the statement "I am" can build us up or destroy us. We must have a heightened self-awareness rooted in self-reflection and personal accountability. Chinese philosopher Lao Tzu once said, watch your thoughts, they become words, words become actions, actions become habits, habits become your character, and your character becomes your destiny. **Our mental health is directly connected to our thoughts, which means our thoughts are the basis for managing our mental health**. Can we really control our thoughts? Yes, with baby steps. The process first begins with us listening to our thoughts and understanding what they mean. If we are having very dark thoughts of hurting someone or ourselves, there is a problem. Even though these thoughts may never turn into actions, the fact that these thoughts entered our mind tells us that there is a problem we need to address.

Let me be completely honest with you; suicidal thoughts have entered my mind and even turned into pleas like "What if I just die?". As I reflected on these dark times—because this was not an isolated moment—I found that I was trying to reassure myself that I did have a purpose in life. That last statement may surprise many people in my life because, outwardly, I never displayed any signs of suicide or even depression. Check on your strong friends because thoughts are silent and many remain private, but if you pay close attention and build deep, meaningful relationships rooted in true friendship, you will see. Typically, when we have these thoughts, we verbalize them to mainly two people: the person we feel is afflicting the most pain and the person we trust the most.

Narcissism is a mental illness, and more often than not, one of the people we express pain to is a narcissist. Remember these words, "hurt people, hurt people." The narcissist could be a parent, a spouse, an enabler friend, or a supervisor. I learned from my children that we are born free and taught to be slaves. Parents play a huge role in the conditioning of the mind that would either make a child more vulnerable to mental illness or not. Although the exact cause of narcissism is not conclusive, our parent's parenting style (either through excessive pampering or criticism) is one of the key factors.

Epigenetics also plays a role in our mental health because, along with the physical genetics we share with our parents, we also share memories dating throughout our ancestral bloodline. As always, I recommend you do research to better understand epigenetics and mental illnesses such as narcissism. Aside from DNA and family relationships, environmental factors impact our mental health. For example, we observe how society glamorizes narcissism. If there is a thin line between love and hate, then there is also a thin line between self-love and narcissism. A narcissist has a high sense of self-importance but also has low self-esteem, or they may be dealing with self-hatred on some level. How does society feed off this narcissism?

Even if the person is not outwardly conceited, they could still be very narcissistic due to extremely low self-esteem. Today's narcissist often displays themselves as a victim. Just look on social media. People are not selling their souls for money; they are selling them for attention. *Likes* replace the characteristics that would make a person likable. Narcissists lack empathy, so if they are playing victim, how much do you think they care about a real victim? They probably think the other person is acting too. Environmental factors literally change the structure and functioning of our brain. As a result, our rewired brain normalizes pain. Humans are the caretakers of *everything* on this earth; it is our nature to care for others who are in need. So what happens to our mind when we go against our instinct?

We are socially engineered to adopt a narcissistic mindset. Consider two examples of this. In the late 80s and 90s, possibly the most highly viewed commercial on TV was the child hunger video. The commercial depicted images of children starving in Africa as a voice-over asked for your donation. As a child, my mom used these commercials to help me appreciate the few things I did have. She'd often say, "Don't waste no food. There are kids starving in Africa." While some people donated to these charities, most of us did not.

If it is our nature to give to others, then we experience a moral dilemma when most people do not help others. What does this lack of harmony do to us mentally? It removes us from our instincts and desensitizes our behavior. Narcissism is rooted in the dehumanization of others and is intent on making oneself feel more important.

If it is our nature to give to others, we experience a moral dilemma when most people do not help others. What does this lack of harmony do to us mentally? It removes us from our instincts and desensitizes our behavior. Narcissism is rooted in the dehumanization of others and is intent on making oneself superior to others.

We may experience this when we pass a homeless person on the street. And I'm from New York, so I know about the homeless hustle that feeds off people's good nature. It would be best to use discernment in everything you do to help others in need. Sometimes you have to ask them what they need. Is it a blanket or some food? Even if you give them some loose change, it's better than looking away as if they don't exist.

## Characteristic of a Narcissist
- Sense of self-importance
- Lack of empathy
- Arrogant behavior
- An excessive urge for admiration
- Strong sense of entitlement

## Human Nature
- Caretakers (helping others is our core role)
- Curiosity (we are explorers and creators)
- Creators (creativity eases the mind)
- Empathic (We are emotional beings.)
- Survival (We survive because of our purpose.)

# Practice Mindfulness and Meditation

"Anything that perverts our human nature is a mental illness."

Fear consistently takes you out of the present. Instead of focusing on the here and now, you are always worried about what could happen in the future. **Worrying about bad things that might happen prevents you from enjoying the good things that are happening now.**

Practicing mindfulness and meditation keeps you firmly rooted in the present. All of your energy and focus is given to the current moment. Simply put, you can be fully present in the present.

Now, to be clear, there is a difference between mindfulness and meditation. Generally speaking, mindfulness simply means being aware of and savoring the present moment without thinking about anything else. You can do any activity mindfully.

When you eat mindfully, you savor every bit, absorbing all the rich flavors you are experiencing. When you jog mindfully, you feel the burn in your muscles and focus on putting one foot in front of the other.

**Mindfulness is a way of life.**

**Meditation is a specific practice that helps you grow in mindfulness.** Although there are many different forms of meditation, they all involve focusing on the present for a set time. Some meditations help you clear your mind, while others promote positive feelings like peace, love, or compassion.

**If you've never practiced meditation, there are numerous tools available that provide expert guidance:**

- **Sound therapy** has a considerable number of guided meditations, sleep sounds, mini-meditations, and more. The modern standard musical frequency is 440 Hz, which is known to distort balance in the body. Most can agree that 440 Hz should be replaced—but there's some argument over which frequency should replace it: 432 Hz or 528 Hz.

- **Breathwork** uses the cadence of your breath to ease your body and release stress.

- **Tantra/Tantric Sex** is an ancient practice that revolves around sexual practices that create a deep, intimate connection. The goal is to be present in the moment to achieve a sensual and fulfilling sexual experience, not an orgasm. For those who are intrigued, we will discuss tantra later in this chapter.

- **Yoga** combines physical mobility and meditation, allowing you to strengthen your body and mind simultaneously.

Breathwork is the most common form of mediation. Mediation is not about sitting still or relaxing; mediation is best defined as the ability to escape the realm of time. When the past, present, and future exist on the current plane, an hour can feel like 15 minutes. Try some guided meditation and breathwork sessions, using some of the resources outlined in the back of this book. Just like with running, controlling your breath is the key to handling stress in the body. **To counteract anxiety, focus on changing your breathing patterns and gaining a rhythm.**

- Inhale slowly through your open mouth, pulling your breath all the way into the back of your skull. Hold the breath for several seconds, then slowly exhale. Repeat this pattern until you feel your anxiety beginning to dissipate. Allow for about 7-10 seconds on both the inhale and exhale. For the best results, do this while laying down or in a relaxed, seated position. Once you've learned to control your breathing, you will be able to maintain these breathing techniques while in an active state of consciousness.

**The more you meditate and practice mindfulness, the less anxiety you'll feel.** Instead of being preoccupied with the past or the future, you have to savor the present, right? Mediation aligns the past, future, and present into the current moment. Einstein once said, "time is an illusion," meaning that time is relative, and the dividing line between the past, the present, and the future is an illusion because reality is timeless.

**What is tantric?** Tantric sex is a slow, meditative form of sex where the end goal is not orgasm but rather to enjoy the sexual journey and body sensations. It aims to move sexual energy throughout the body for the purpose of healing, transformation, and enlightenment.

Proponents of tantric sex believe that tantric techniques may help resolve sexual complications such as premature ejaculation, erectile dysfunction, or anorgasmia.

Tantric sex encourages people to get to know their bodies and become in tune with them. By understanding your body's desires, you can incorporate tantric techniques during sex with a partner. Tantric sex may lead to greater sexual fulfillment and more intense orgasms.

It can be useful to engage in tantric self-love or masturbation without orgasm to understand your body's wants.

Sexual energy is the most powerful energy that we exchange. Sex magic is real, but most of us don't tap into this powerful energy because we misuse our sexual energy. Don't be scared by the word magic—is it not magic that a tiny sperm cell enters into an egg and creates new life? When you ejaculate or have an orgasm, you release the energy of creation. A child is not the only thing created through sexual intercourse; with each orgasm comes the power of manifestation. This is why mediation is such an essential practice; it helps us stay focused. If you go into sex with the sole goal of having an orgasm, you lose sight of the things you can truly manifest. You birth ideas through sex by focusing on the things you want to produce up until the climax.

Tantric sex is more powerful when you set intentions together with your partner. If you are not creating something, an orgasm is just a form of instant, short-term gratification. Frequent masturbation, especially through the use of porn, can be counterproductive to our ability to create. The lights from a phone or TV put our mind into a trance state of receiving mode rather than the producing mode.

Semen retention is similar to detoxing or fasting, which allows the body to heal and reset. You can harness your sexual energy by refraining from ejaculation for 30 days.

"No Nut November" is 30 days of no ejaculation, allowing the body to redirect that energy inward. Semen retention is typically done during the winter months because winter is also the season of increased depression. During this time, people experience higher rates of seasonal depression; when old habits die, we have to let go of things to prosper in the next season.

Immediately after ejaculation, our body goes into *mission complete* mode, like a washing machine after it completes a washing cycle and turns off. Our minds go into a reflection period. For many of us, we can go into an emotional state of guilt, shame, or regret whether the ejaculation stems from masturbation or a sexual partner. Tantra provides us with an enjoyable alternative. I encourage you to research the history of tantra and the variety of tantra practices before your first experience.

∴

As a young man, I often found that I became wiser after an orgasm, gaining a close observation of my environment that I had missed out on in pursuit of an orgasm. Ejaculation hangover is the numbness of emotion that can linger after this release. During the next seven days, we go into our comfort state of homeostasis, which differs from person to person. Typically, a man under 35 takes three days to replenish the nutrients he loses during ejaculation, while men over 40 take about eight days. By the end of the 7th day, you experience increased energy, clarity, and motivation compiled with your body's recharging.

During Day 8 through Day 14, the body goes through a testing process, and this will be your most challenging week. Your body will feel the pressure to release itself, and as your sexual desire rises, your sexual endurance will fall. At this stage, you are developing will power, and as you push through this week, your body will integrate that energy back into the production cycle of the body aura. When people say you are glowing, it represents this sexual energy moving inward and reflecting outwardly.

Days 15 through 21 are when the power shifts back into your control, and you internalize energy. Throughout this week, you will find true alignment as you begin to identify the psychosocial issues that influence your life. Your sexual endurance will begin to increase as you take more control over this sexual energy.

Days 22 through 30 are when you develop new baseline homeostasis that aligns with your true nature. The powerful energy of the previous week becomes peaceful and gentle. A sense of easeful relief is maintained as the body heals from within. During this stage of the process, the body absorbs this sexual energy, increasing the creative and productive power of any individual.

## SEMEN RETENTION PROCESS

**Post Ejaculation:** Mission Complete, Reflection Period, Non Peak Performance, Ejaculation Hangover

**1-7 Days:** Baseline Homeostasis, Energy Boost, Clarity Boost, Motivation Boost, Charging Body

**8-14 Days**: Pressure, Willpower, Integration, Radiate, Heighten Sexual Desire

**15-21 Days:** Power, Alignment, Psychosocial, Presence, Sex Endurance increase

**22-30 Days:** Sovereignty, Easeful Power, Shifted Baseline Homeostasis, Embodied Presence

# HAVE A FIVE-YEAR PLAN

"Everyone has a plan until they get punched in the face." Mike Tyson

One of the big challenges in dealing with fear is that it's always present. At any moment, worries can crowd into your mind, disrupting your day, stealing your energy, and making it difficult to be present.

On top of this, many people find it difficult to turn their brains off. Once anxiety has wormed its way into their minds, they can't stop thinking about it. As a result, the same fears circle in their brains again and again. It's a vicious cycle that can be difficult to break.

One technique recommended by psychologists is scheduling a time when you will think about the things that worry you.

**It works like this:**

- Set aside 15-30 minutes every day.

- During that time, write down everything that worries you. You don't have to create solutions. You just need to get things down on paper.

- If you start to worry about something at any other point in the day, tell yourself that you will think about it during your "worry time."

In the beginning, you may find it challenging to put off your worries, but **over time it will become easier.** Your control over your mind will increase, and you'll find it less difficult to clamp down on your swirling mind.

An additional benefit of planned worry is that **it increases your sense of control over your life.** Though you may not be able to control the circumstances that are causing your fears, you can decide exactly when you want to think about them.

In 2012, the Department of Veterans Affairs' conducted a study on veteran suicide and concluded that **22 veterans a day die by suicide due to Post Trauma Stress Disorder (PTSD)**. That's 8,030 veterans annually from all war eras, including Korean, WW2, Vietnam, Afghanistan, and Iraq. This amounts to more suicides in one year than the total number of American lives lost during both Operation Enduring Freedom (Afghanistan) and Operation Iraqi Freedom. This is an alarming number, and many people may find it hard to believe. Yet, these numbers are a stark reality.

- Depression
- Self-blame for mission failure
- Survivor's guilt
- An altered worldview due to post-traumatic stress
- Impaired thinking caused by alcohol or substance abuse
- Traumatic brain injury or another life-changing injury

These are just a few examples of reasons why a veteran might take their own life.

So, why is having a plan vital? Plans help us put things into perspective. Remember, fear is perception based, so knowledge applied from perspective helps us make practical decisions. Perception without perspective is instability in all areas of life. When you join a new group, a team, a job, or an organization, there is always something you have to figure out.

I would always tell my newest recruits that there was a blueprint to success. I learned this from having five siblings. In a large family, you learn the rules of the game before you play. See, the rules to the game are the blueprint, and from there, you build your strategy. Most of us dive into things without knowing the rules and wonder why we can't win in the game. If you don't know the rules, someone could easily create *house* rules to give themselves a greater advantage. Your plan is developed by determining your desired end goal. This strategy is called reverse planning, where you outline what you would like to achieve and build a plan to accomplish it. This is where the five-year plan comes into play.

The five-year plan is designed to help you develop your current job skills or prepare you for your next job. Your five-year plan is very much an individual and personal plan designed to facilitate your growth, development, and career advancement. Once you prepare your plan, meet with your supervisor, mentor, a family member, or another supportive individual to gain the feedback needed to achieve your goals. Always use the SMART model when setting goals: **Specific, Measurable, Attainable, Realistic, and within a specific Timeframe.**

Another less formal option is creating a vision board. This project could be done individually or in groups with your family or team. This visualization tool encompasses a board of any sort used to build a collage of words and pictures representing your goals and dreams.

∴

While serving as a platoon sergeant, I created a simple, yet highly effective vision board based on the Army semi-centralized promotion point system. Every Soldiers' name was added to the board as a table chart with categories showing how many points each soldier had. We updated the board daily as soldiers gained more points, and also at the end of the week, to highlight the Soldier with the most points prominently at the top. To this day, many of these Soldiers may not even realize that as a team, we built a collective vision board; the results of this project were staggering. In six months, the Army promoted 67% of the Soldiers classified as 25V in the grade of E4 to E5. While at the same time promoting 33% of the Soldiers classified as 25V in the grade of E5 to E6. All of these promotions occurred in just one platoon. I saw firsthand how planning gave these remarkable Soldiers a purpose.

In 2015, I set a SMART goal to write my first leadership book by the end of 2020. *Mental Health Now* is a tangible product of that plan. Although things won't always go exactly how you plan, you have to keep moving closer and closer towards your goals. A plan helps reinforce your purpose, and purpose is the reason we keep moving forward. We can endure pain when there is a purpose for it.

*"How can we develop anyone without first knowing their plan?" - Christopher Adell*

# CIRCLE OF INFLUENCE

"You can't change the people around you, but you can change the people you choose to be around."

Dealing with fear is a lonely battle, often waged just in your mind. Most people around you have no idea what you're dealing with, especially if you still maintain an external appearance of wellness.

Moreover, it is difficult to discern whether your fears are reasonable or simply the product of your imagination. **This is why getting support from others is crucial if you regularly worry.**

When you tell others what you're thinking, you'll get to look at your worries from a different perspective. You can also receive encouragement and clarity. You'll find that your support circle can often shine light into the darkness of your fears.

**Some ways to get needed support are:**

1. **Talk to a friend.** Unburden yourself to someone that you know well and can trust. This person should be completely accepting of you and not think that your fears are silly, no matter how small these fears are.

2. **Join an online support group.** There are many online organizations specifically designed to help you cope with anxiety, including:

   - ○ <u>Turn2Me</u>
   - ○ <u>Anxiety and Depression Association of America</u>
   - ○ <u>7 Cups of Tea</u>
   - ○ <u>Daily Strength</u>

3. **Join a local support group.** Depending on where you live, there may be in-person anxiety support groups that you can join.

**Don't be embarrassed if you struggle with serious fear.** Every person has their share of worries and anxieties. You're not any different, and you're not alone. Talking to others about your struggles can go a long way in helping you make progress. It can lighten the load you're carrying.

Maya Angelou once said:

*Each one of us has lived through some devastation, some loneliness, some weather superstorm or spiritual superstorm, when we look at each other we must say, I understand. I understand how you feel because I have been there myself. We must support each other and empathize with each other because each of us is more alike than we are unalike.*

When you get support from others, you feel empathy and understanding. This can give you the strength you need to keep fighting.

∴

Earlier in this book, we discussed the five fingers of human relationships, but we have two hands and ten fingers. Your other hand represents your non-dominant hand. These are the five friendships that influence you the most. These friendships could be with leaders, mentors, other family members, close associates, and even siblings. In some cases, we can be influenced by people we consider to be our enemy. **When you are experiencing**

**mental health issues, you often love people who maintain you in your self-destruction, and more often than not, your friends are your worst enemies.** Who are the five people who have the most influence on your life?

Remember, you are the average of the sum of the five people who most influence you. Influence is the capacity to affect the character, development, or behavior of someone. I tell my oldest daughter when her little sister copies her that mimicking is the highest form of flattery. This is true in adulthood too. This is why I would always come up with phrases and sayings to feed others' subconscious minds. Over time, they would find themselves reciting these phrases, and this would confirm that I was influencing them on a deeper level. The subconscious mind is programmed in three main ways; symbols, repetition, and trauma. This is why musicians have so much influence on people; the repetition of creative expression is powerful.

If five average people influence you, you will be average, and rarely are there any exceptions to this rule. In most cases, it doesn't take removing all five people from your circle to see growth; changing one person can spark the change you need to get to the next level. I made it my goal to be that one person in someone else's circle of influence who helped them stretch, allowing them to grow and become the best version of themselves.

Looking back at my life, almost all of the people within my circle of influence have exceeded expectations: friends, business partners, and subordinates alike. Being a visionary is seeing what you want to happen and making it manifest. There is power in seeing the good in people, even when they are not in their best form; we all have greatness within us. As influencers, we have to change the way we look at others copying us. If you copy me, I want to give you the entire blueprint so you can make it your own. As you influence others, they influence others, and this is how building legacies begin.

"Good artists borrow, great artist steal" Pablo Picasso

# TALK WITH A THERAPIST, LIFE COACH OR MENTOR
### "Talk to me"

If you struggle with significant amounts of fear regularly, consider talking with a therapist. Therapists or coaches can help you identify what you're afraid of and then guide you forward.

Using both their extensive training and experience, **they can give you specific exercises that will help you overcome your fears.**

Therapists can be especially helpful if you struggle with phobias, like fear of flying or dogs. These trained professionals are equipped with proven techniques like exposure therapy and cognitive behavioral therapy. They can help you overcome issues that may have hampered you for years.

**How do you know if you should go to a therapist?** The American Psychological Association (2017) posed these questions:

- *Do you or someone close to you spend some amount of time every week thinking about the problem?*
- *Is the problem embarrassing, to the point that you want to hide from others?*

- *Over the past few months, has the problem reduced your quality of life?*
- *Does the problem take up considerable time (e.g., more than an hour per day)?*
- *Have you curtailed your work or educational ambitions because of the problem?*
- *Are you rearranging your lifestyle to accommodate the problem?*

If you answered "yes" to any of these questions, then you would probably benefit from seeing a therapist, life coach, or counselor.

When it comes to finding a therapist or coach, you have several options. First, you can find one locally. If you don't know of a good local therapist, Psychology Today has a searchable directory (https://www.psychologytoday.com/us/therapists), and the International Coaching Federation has a coach finder (https://coachfederation.org/find-a-coach)

There are also numerous online therapy options available. Most of these online options offer both video sessions and text chat.

Therapists will also try to work with your insurance provider to ensure that the support you need is also affordable.

**For more counseling support, check out these websites:**

- Betterhelp (http://www.betterhelp.com)
- Talkspace (http://www.talkspace.com)
- Amwell (http://www.amwell.com)
- DoctorOnDemand (http://www.doctorondemand.com)
- MDLive (http://www.mdlive.com)

Unfortunately, there is often a stigma surrounding therapy or coaching; a person who sees a therapist is considered weak somehow like they weren't strong enough to deal with their own challenges.

Don't buy into this idea. **Many of the strongest, most successful people in the world go to therapy.** CEOs, professional athletes, and military leaders have therapists or coaches. If they can benefit, you can too. Since 2018, I've used behavioral health as a means to manage my mental health. Leaders must take care of themselves because if you can't take care of yourself, how can you truly take care of others.

∴

Finding the right mentor is key to long term success and fulfillment in life. No man is an island, alone you go fast, but together you go far. Choose your mentor wisely but understand there is no perfect mentor, and everyone is fallible.

I've made many mistakes in life, but I continue to look at each day as an opportunity to learn and grow. I made some mistakes privately while others on the public stage. I remember when I was dropped from the Master Fitness Training (MFT) course in 2013 because I had too much pride and refused to go to the doctor to get my knee checked. In 2016, I failed to plan for a company land navigation course and delegated the task without adequate supervision. These are just a few of the many mistakes I've made in my career, but in life I've made many more. It's not always easy to take accountability for failure, but only through failure are we truly able to grow. The most important thing for a leader or anyone in a position of authority to understand is that "we must expect a reasonable amount of failure from our subordinates." Perfection as a construct is an illusion; we have to learn to find perfection in the imperfections. We are not infallible.

A mentor and a mentee's relationship is not one-sided; a great mentor will always learn from their mentee. Iron sharpens iron, so one person sharpens another. Every person that I've mentored has helped me grow into a better man because I was teachable. Like this book, instead of telling a mentee what they should do, I've provided real-life examples that allow the gift of discernment to be used. Although they may still come to me seeking advice and answers, I rarely ever left them with my opinion as a response.

My philosophy on mentorship is "just as you come is just as you go." If you come to me with a question, I will send you off with a question to answer yourself. I am a mirror. I don't see myself as someone who just pours into others. Yes, as a mentor, you will train, teach, and learn, but that only captures the surface level of mentorship. The best mentors pull what is already inside someone and bring it to the surface. Many of us have our true greatness buried under pain, trauma, pride, ego, insecurity, and other things we are afraid of. This act of pulling greatness to the surface allows an individual to manifest their true nature. Many of the people I mentored realized that the things they were doing were not in alignment with who they were, and therefore these individuals often changed what they were doing. Remember, all change comes from within, so ultimately it is our own responsibility to change.

Once you reveal who you are to yourself, there is no going back. In the conscious community, I tell people that there is no *unwoke* button. To mentor someone in this way, you have to get to know them personally and not just read information about them from a cue card. If your mentee doesn't consider you a friend, then you are not close enough to help them. **Friendship is not toxic in leadership, but the lack of true connection allows toxic leadership to exist.** The biggest obstacle to making this connection is the lack of discipline and the presence of judgment. It is unlikely that a person will share their weaknesses if they feel they will be faced with judgment. It is also detrimental for a mentor to get close to a mentee if they lack the discipline necessary to maintain professional behavior. Fortunately, I've never made this mistake. Yet, I understand the psychology behind it. Admiration could easily turn into a deeper infatuation, whether it's a teacher and a student, a supervisor and an employee, or a leader and a subordinate; making this relationship unprofessional would jeopardize the mentor and mentee bond. Honestly, we see this happen a lot. To prevent this, mentors have to gain awareness of how and when to set boundaries. We are all fallible, but knowing your strengths and weaknesses will allow you to make the best judgment calls about what situations you put yourself in.

# HAVE
# SELF-LOVE

"My first love is myself."

It's essential to remember that you're not defective if you regularly experience fear and anxiety. Many factors contribute to fear, including:

- Biology
- Genetics
- Experience
- Environment
- Current circumstances
- Epigenetics (or family history)

Any one of these things can cause you to feel afraid. It's not as though you're choosing to be fearful because you like it.

**In light of this, be compassionate toward yourself.** Don't try to deny the existence of your fears or act like you have it all together. Accept and love yourself, your fears, and all.

If you're unwilling to accept yourself until you completely overcome your fears, you'll be perpetually unhappy. The reality is that fear will never be completely absent from your life. Even the most courageous people in the world feel anxiety from time to time.

If you want to overcome fear, you must have the courage first to accept yourself as you are. Sociologist Brene Brown said, *"I now see how owning our story and loving ourselves through that process is the bravest thing that we will ever do."*

Own your story. Own the factors that cause fear to arise in you and own the actions necessary to calm those fears. The lack of self-love is the clearest sign of a mental health issue. Someone dealing with self-hatred is not automatically suicidal. Self-hatred could be caused by systemic things like institutional racism or environmental problems such as poverty or a lack of family stability. Self-hatred is connected to a deep trauma that has not been healed, and if it is tethered to one of the five human relationships on either hand, it could be amplified. When you unpackage the trauma of self-hatred, you are likely to see one of two responses;

- You become the person that you feel inflicted this trauma on you.
- You destroy anyone who presents the characteristics of the person who inflicted this trauma on you.

In both responses, the behavior is not productive, and the eye for an eye method will not heal you.

Love is the great equalizer and not just love for another person, but love for yourself and your passion. We were all put here to love—love ourselves, love others, and love what we do. We are creators by nature, and when someone is not resonating on the frequency of love, it's likely because they are not doing what they love. Just as one male sperm enters into a female egg and creates a baby, life is inside creation, and creation is love.

∴

Why is poverty strongly connected to self-hatred? The lack of ability to create the things they want. Television shows us all the new and shiny things that we can't have, and it could limit what we feel is possible. Like me, most kids who grew up in the inner-city wanted to be a rapper, actor, or athlete, which was like winning the lottery. Every year about a million boys want to make it into the NBA, and of that million, only 400,000 will make it to play high school basketball. Of that 400,000, only 4,000 will make it to play college basketball. Of that 4,000, only 35 will make it into the NBA. Of that 35, only seven will start, and the NBA's average career is only four years. So, we have a million boys fighting for seven full-time jobs that will only last for about four years.

Extracurricular activities like basketball severely aid in managing mental health because they have been systematically programmed into our minds as a way out of childhood trauma. I was once questioned and criticized by my partner for spending 3 to 4 hours in the gym on Saturdays playing basketball or traveling on the weekends to play basketball with the post team. I thought I was just working out my body, but I was also managing my mental health. The same rules apply to some people over 35 who are still making and producing music; this is mental health management, and it should be seen as such whether they make it to the professional level or not.

I had an opportunity to volunteer at an inpatient mental health treatment center, leading a small group while they participated in art therapy. What I saw was pain leaving the body and joy entering into it as they created artwork. The creation of a masterpiece can hold the same emotions as birthing a child. If you think I'm lying, check out the scene from the movie *Hustle and Flow* when Djay gave his recorded music tape to Skinny Black, and Skinny dropped it into the toilet. Djay beat the breaks off of Skinny, someone he looked up to. Sometimes the best thing you can do for someone is to help them find their passion.

# BE FEARLESS

"Be fearless in the pursuit of what sets your soul on fire."

Courage is not the absence of fear. A person who never feels fear isn't courageous. They're crazy. The world can be a pretty scary place, and there are lots of reasons to feel afraid.

**Courage is feeling afraid and acting anyway.** Courageous people acknowledge their fears and then move forward to overcome them.

Nelson Mandela said it this way:

> *I learned that courage was not the absence of fear, but the triumph over it. The brave man is not he who does not feel afraid, but he who conquers that fear.*

It's okay to feel fear or worry but avoid letting them get the best of you. Don't let anxiety keep you from living the life of your dreams.

**We've talked about several different ways to deal with fear and worry:**

- Change your biology
- Identify your fears
- Practice worst-case and best-case thinking

- Focus on what you can control
- Choose gratitude
- Practice mindfulness and meditation
- Schedule your worries
- Get support
- Talk to a therapist
- Have self-compassion

These techniques won't eliminate fear from your life, but they will make it easier for you to cope with it.

Make no mistake—it's not easy to overcome fear. It takes consistent work. You must have the courage to come face-to-face with the things that truly frighten you. You have to expend energy to get your thoughts under control.

**But the work is worth it.** As a result, you will experience freedom, peace, and confidence. Circumstances won't easily rattle you. You'll know that you can handle whatever comes your way. A wonderful, adventurous future awaits you. You just need to step forward and take it.

∴

I was one year into my contract in the army, stationed at Fort Bliss. I wanted the freedom to live off base and have my own apartment, so I decided to rent a room from a co-worker. Barely old enough to drink, I yearned to live a life free and independent from the control of the military. Yet, I was too inexperienced to recognize the mental tools I needed to find peace, and so I chased whatever I thought would bring it.

I've only shared this story with one other person. Men may be familiar with the concept of "taking one for the team." It is a brotherhood code that holds you responsible for running interference while someone on your team pursues a woman. Your responsibilities often include entertaining or distracting her friend, so your friend can make a play or hookup. Some men have a theory that there is always one woman who is significantly less attractive than her friends in every group of women. This woman's mood impacts the outcome of how events play out as she can end all potential hookups by saying four words, "It's time to go." I was never good at the interference role as I could not fake interest in a woman I was not attracted to.

One night my roommate, who I also considered a friend, invited a woman over, and she brought a friend. That night was her first time at our place, so I understood why she brought a friend. The problem was I wasn't down for entertaining her friend. So I told my roommate that I would drink with them, but I'd be dry. What happened that night occurred earlier in the same year Quickley died. Both experiences serve as powerful lessons I learned early in life about alcohol. Today, they remain the basis for my decision not to drink alcohol.

I had zero interest in her friend. I found her to be completely unattractive. She was loud, obnoxious, and pushy. At one point during the night, she rubbed her body against mine and damn near backed me into a corner just to get close to me. Now I can sleep through gunfire, and so sleepy and drunk were a bad combination for me. As I was sitting on the couch, my roommate and his girl left to go to his bedroom. Her friend stayed behind. She was seated on the other side of the sofa where I was sitting. As she was talking, I dozed off.

I woke up moments later to her giving me oral sex. I immediately jumped up in shock and quickly pulled up my pants. I couldn't even say anything to her. I just pointed at her and then walked to the bathroom to wash myself off. As I cleaned myself off, tears started falling from my eyes. All I could think was, *what the hell just happened.* This traumatic event was my first experience with oral sex, and I knew I didn't consent to it in any way. I questioned myself on whether or not I enjoyed it because women can't sexually assault men. Back then, I was misled to believe that only women were victims of sexual assault. Later that day, I would experience firsthand what perpetuated the basis for that lie.

**Until now, I have only told one person about what happened to me that night.** It wasn't my roommate, my leadership, or my family because I was too embarrassed. The one person I told was the last person I thought would judge me. And although he didn't judge me, he laughed. He laughed at me so hard that it made me suck my tears back into my eyes and bury that pain. That pain quickly turned into anger, and eventually, I found a reason to unfriend my roommate and simultaneously destroy his character through a diss record called "Ether 2.0".

He had used me to get this girl and her friend to come over by saying I was down to go all the way or, in male terms, "take one for the team." I felt betrayed, angry, and had a vengeful heart. Fighting him wouldn't have been good enough. I wanted to humiliate him, the same way I felt he did me.

When you're dealing with mental health issues, you often lack empathy, which allows you to justify toxic behaviors as a means to solve problems. Looking back now, I regret how I handled the situation because, at the end of the day, my roommate wasn't the one who violated me. I had to take responsibility for not changing the environment I was in—no matter who took advantage of me. **It was not my fault what happened to me, but I was responsible for how I allowed it to affect me.** I had to realize that the pain I felt then would last forever if I allowed it to, and I was the only person who could change how I felt.

Mental slavery is when you feel as if you don't have a choice. Once you realize that you always have a choice, you are no longer a slave. You may not find it easy to make the right choice, but survival is in our nature. We can quickly turn pain into passion, but passion alone can be destructive if we let our pain guide us. You must connect your passion to a purpose, and purpose is best executed with a plan.

Often in the moment, victims can't even face their real perpetrators because the pain associated with their trauma is overwhelming. I will always remember her name and her face, even though I only saw her once. The memory of that traumatic event is programmed into my mind. And holding onto the pain has only held me back, but now I am in the final stage of my healing process. In this stage, it is not about revenge or holding her accountable; it is about awareness and sharing my story so others can learn from it.

In some ways, this painful experience made me feel ashamed of my body and hindered me from owning my sexual energy. Tantric helped me to become free sexually and heal. The sexual assault happened in 2005 when I was only 21 years old. Since then, I've found myself in situations where people required the highest level of trust from me. There were women with whom I shared a mutual attraction. We partied together, and they drank too much. I saw myself as a protector and put my attraction aside to ensure that these women were safe. I've been the designated driver for female co-workers who trusted me, although I didn't fully understand why they had given me their trust. I had someone confide in me about the sexual assault they experienced as a child, and I was the first person they ever told. A few others started to confide in me but then stopped out of shame, fear, or guilt. I'll always remember these moments and understand the pain they felt even without words being expressed.

Since 2005, my five most impactful, intimate relationships (whether a marriage or committed relationship) have had one thing in common. Of these women, all five of them were sexually assaulted. There is no coincidence that I formed relationships with these women. I've developed a protective spirit and am attracted to women who need to be protected. For many years, I felt obligated to protect my partners, and over time this left me unprotected. Protecting others is essential, but you must always protect yourself first to be most effective.

In 2012, I had my first daughter, Chrislyn, and in 2018 my youngest daughter, Ahsha, was born. My daughters have helped me shift my focus inward and heal so that I can help them throughout their journey. To protect others, we must first create a protective environment for ourselves. To illustrate, when you get on a plane, the flight attendant instructs you to put your oxygen mask on first before you help others when faced with an emergency. Your physical and mental well-being is essential to helping others.

This book can help you identify your mental health's current state, so you can be in the best position to help others. Each chapter connects to a story or part of my life that I had to work through. You can use each chapter to reflect on your life—the past, the present, and the future simultaneously. Connecting the dots from these points in your life can help you see your end game. I will leave you with three questions to reflect on.

*What is your passion? (Past)*

*What is your purpose? (Present)*

*What is your plan? (Future)*

# Resources and links

- Turn2Me ( https://turn2me.org/group-supports)
- Anxiety and Depression (https://adaa.org/adaa-online-support-groupAssociation of America)
- 7 Cups of Tea (https://www.7cups.com/)
- Daily Strength (https://www.dailystrength.org/group/anxiety)
- Betterhelp (http://www.betterhelp.com)
- Talkspace (http://www.talkspace.com)
- Amwell (http://www.amwell.com)
- DoctorOnDemand (http://www.doctorondemand.com)
- MDLive (http://www.mdlive.com)
- www.holisticallyhealarious.com
- Tantra Challenge: (www.learnwithjahsun.com)
- Untitled Production Video (PMR and guided meditation)(47) Untitled Production Team GW Apparel - YouTube
- Psychology Today has a searchable directory (https://www.psychologytoday.com/us/therapists), International Coaching Federation has a coach finder (https://coachfederation.org/find-a-coach)